Sue Stratford owns and runs The Knitting Hut, a yarn and needle supplier, and she finds the yarns she stocks there and her customers a constant source of inspiration. She teaches knitting and crochet workshops as well as offering advice to customers, and loves sharing her skills with others. She always has countless knitting projects on the go. Sue lives in Milton Keynes with her husband and five children.

Knitted Meerkats

Knitted Meerkats

Sue Stratford

Search Press

First published in Great Britain 2012

Search Press Limited
Wellwood, North Farm Road,
Tunbridge Wells, Kent TN2 3DR

Text copyright © Sue Stratford 2012

Photographs by Debbie Patterson and Paul Bricknell
at Search Press Studios

Photographs and design copyright © Search Press Ltd 2012

ISBN 978 1 84448 774 5

Suppliers
If you have difficulty in obtaining any of the materials and
equipment mentioned in this book, then please visit the
Search Press website for details of suppliers:
www.searchpress.com

Materials can also be obtained from the author's
own website:
www.theknittinghut.co.uk

Printed in China

Dedication
This book is dedicated to my fabulous family,
who have giggled and laughed at all these
designs and always give me their most honest
opinion, whether I want it or not!

Acknowledgements
I would like to thank everyone at Team Hut for their
help and support with this book, especially Lucy,
Phyl, Babs, Heather, Bekky, Claire, Janet and Pippa.
Without you this would not have been possible!
Thanks also go to Designer Yarns for their kind
donation of yarn for these projects.

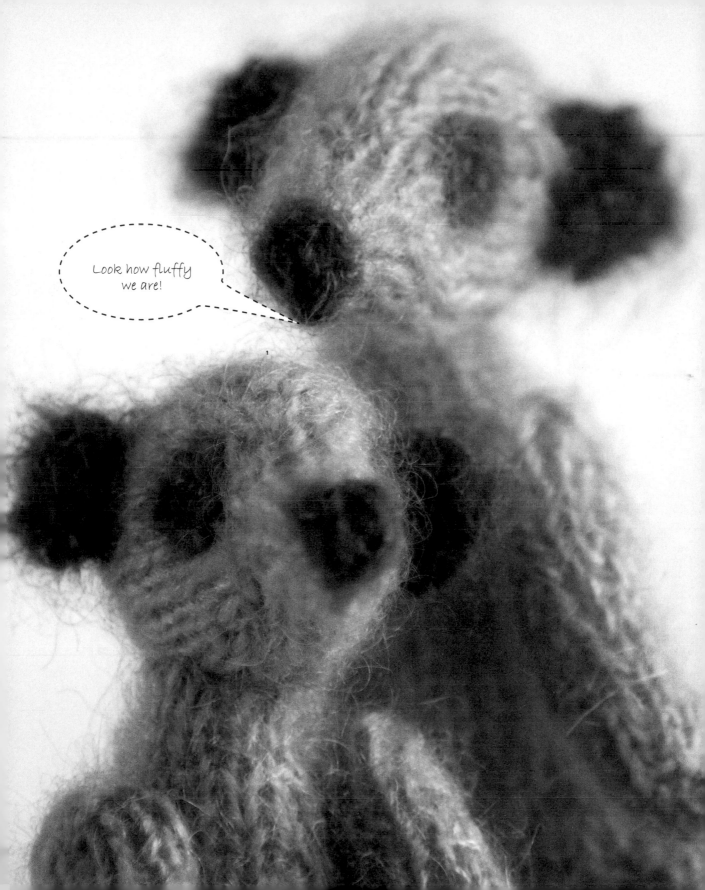

Contents

Skier-Kat

Flower Power

Soccer Star

Wedding Belle

Beach Babe

Prima Ballerina

Fluffy Flippers

Baby Meerkat

The Count

Santa Paws

Meerkat Clan

Bollywood

Acrobat Kats

School for Kats

Meer Punk

Musical Meerkat

Top Hat and Tail

Cute Bridesmaid

The Sky's the Limit

Prehistoric Kat

Introduction

Everyone loves meerkats. Funny, inquisitive and very, very cute, each little meerkat has his or her own personality and they bring a smile to everyone's face.

The meerkats are knitted with a double strand of fine, fluffy yarn using small needles and feel gorgeous when they are made up. Using fine yarn ensures that you get great detail and expression. The outfits are all knitted in 4-ply (fingering) yarn and are quick and easy to make. Take your time when sewing them together as a lot of the detail is achieved in the finishing. I have used a darning needle for this, and if any other needles have been used they are listed under 'materials'.

Some patterns include a small amount of crochet, but for those of you who do not crochet, alternative methods are given in each case.

Many of the outfits are made so they can be taken on and off easily. You can therefore knit your meerkat an entire wardrobe of

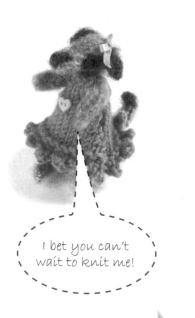

I bet you can't wait to knit me!

8

clothes and accessories. Other outfits are best sewn on to give the best possible finish.

The adult meerkats are 14cm (5½in) high and the babies just 7cm (2¾in) tall. I had great fun choosing the outfits they should wear and the list was so long it was very difficult to choose just twenty. All are equally popular with my family and friends, but I have to confess that the little meerkat dressed up as a dinosaur has to be my favourite! Of course, all the patterns in the book can be adapted by altering the colours or yarns used, or mix-and-matched to create outfits of your own. Make a special, personalised gift for a friend or relative. The baby meerkats make wonderful bag charms or key fobs, and I can't wait to see the bride and groom gracing the top of a wedding cake!

Any tricky techniques are explained and they really help make these little creatures look extra special. To make the meerkats stand up easily I placed two 2.5cm (1in) diameter coins in the base of the body before sewing it up.

I hope you have as much fun making your own mini meerkat (or an entire meerkat clan!) as I did, and choosing a special outfit for them all.

Turn the page to find out how to make us!

9

How to knit a meerkat

Materials

Beige lace-weight yarn (used double throughout)

Dark brown lace-weight yarn (used double throughout)

Toy filling

Two black beads

Chenille stick

Black sewing cotton

Sewing needle

Two 2.5cm (1in) diameter coins

Needles

1 pair of 2.75mm (UK 12, US 2) knitting needles

This is how tall I really am!

14cm (5½in)

Instructions

Remember to use yarn double throughout.

Head

Using beige yarn, cast on 8 sts and, starting with a knit row, work 4 rows in SS.

Next row: K3, (M1, K1) to last 3 sts, M1, K3 [11 sts].

Purl 1 row.

Rep the last 2 rows once more [17 sts].

Work as follows (purl all WS rows):

Row 1: K3, M1, K4, M1, K3, M1, K4, M1, K3 [21 sts].

Row 3: K9, M1, K3, M1, K9 [23 sts].

Row 5: K9, M1, K5, M1, K9 [25 sts].

Next row: K17, K2togtbl, K1, turn.

For the next 3 rows you will be working over part of the row only.

Next row: sl1, P10, P2tog, P1, turn.

Next row: sl1, K11, K2togtbl, K1, turn.

Next row: sl1, P12, P2tog, purl to end of row [21 sts].

Next row: K6, cast off 9 sts, knit to end of row [12 sts].

Starting with a purl row, work 2 rows in SS over the first 6 sts.

**Starting with a purl row, cast off 2 sts, work to end of row.

Work 1 row.

Next row: Cast off 2 sts, work to end of row.

Work 1 row.

Cast off rem 2 sts.

With RS facing, rejoin yarn to rem 6 sts. Starting with a knit row, work 2 rows in SS.

Work from ** to match other side of head.

Body

Using beige yarn, cast on 10 sts and work 4 rows in SS.

Next row: K1, (M1, K2) 4 times, M1, K1 [15 sts].

Work 3 rows in SS.

Next row: K4, M1, K3, M1, K1, M1, K3, M1, K4 [19 sts].

Purl 1 row.

Next row: K4, M1, K11, M1, K4 [21 sts].

Purl 1 row.

Next row: K9, M1, K3, M1, K9 [23 sts].

Work 3 rows in SS.

Next row: K9, M1, K5, M1, K9 [25 sts].

Purl 1 row.

Next row: K9, M1, K7, M1, K9 [27 sts].

Work 3 rows in SS.

Next row: K9, M1, K9, M1, K9 [29 sts].

Work 3 rows in SS.

Next row: K9, M1, K11, M1, K9 [31 sts].

Work 11 rows in SS.

Next row: K1, (K2tog, K2) to last 6 sts, (K2tog, K1) twice [23 sts].

Purl 1 row.

Next row: Cast off 8 sts, K1, Kfb 3 times, K2, cast off 8 sts [10 sts].

Next row (WS): rejoin yarn to rem sts and, starting with a purl row, work 5 rows in SS.

Dec 1 st at beg and end of next 3 rows [4 sts].

Cast off rem sts.

Arms (make two)

Using beige yarn, cast on 6 sts and work 2 rows in SS.

Next row: K1, M1, K4, M1, K1 [8 sts].

Work 3 rows in SS.

* K5, w&t.

P2, w&t.

Knit to end of row [8 sts].

Purl 1 row.

Rep from * once more.

Work as follows (purl all WS rows):

Row 1: K1, M1, K2, K2tog, K2, M1, K1 [9 sts].

Row 3: K1, M1, K3, M1, K1, M1, K3, M1, K1 [13 sts].

Row 5: K1, ssk, K1, ssk, K1, K2tog, K1, K2tog, K1 [9 sts].

Row 7: K1, ssk, sl1, K2tog, psso, K2tog, K1 [5 sts].

Next row (RS): thread yarn through rem sts and fasten.

Right leg

**Using beige yarn, cast on 6 sts and work 2 rows in SS.

Next row: K1, M1, K to last st, M1, K1 [8 sts].

Starting with a purl row, work 9 rows in SS.**

Next row: cast off 3 sts, K1, M1, knit to last st, M1, K1 [7 sts].

Next row: P1, M1, purl to last st, M1, P1 [9 sts].

Next row: K1, M1, knit to last st, M1, K1 [11 sts].

Next row: P1, M1, purl to last st, M1, P1 [13 sts].

Work 4 rows in SS.

*Next row: K1, ssk, knit to last 3 sts, K2tog, K1*** [11 sts].

Purl 1 row.*

Rep from * to * twice more [7 sts].

Rep from * to *** once more [5 sts].

Next row: P2tog, P1, P2tog [3 sts].

Cast off rem sts.

Left leg

Follow instructions for right leg from ** to **.

Knit 1 row.

Next row: cast off 3 sts, P1, M1, P to last st, M1, P1 [7 sts].

Next row: K1, M1, knit to last st, M1, K1 [9 sts].

Next row: P1, M1, purl to last st, M1, P1 [11 sts].

Next row: K1, M1, knit to last st, M1, K1 [13 sts].

Work 4 rows in SS.

*Next row (WS): P1, ssp, purl to last 3 sts, P2tog, P1*** [11 sts].

Knit 1 row.*

Rep from * to * twice more and then from * to *** once more [5 sts].

Next row: K2tog, K1, K2tog [3 sts].

Cast off rem sts.

Tail

Using beige yarn, cast on 8 sts and work 12 rows in SS.

Next row: K1, ssk, knit to last 3 sts, K2tog, K1 [6 sts].

Work 11 rows in SS.

Next row: K1, ssk, K2tog, K1 [4 sts].

Purl 1 row.

Change to dark brown.

Work 4 rows in SS.

Next row: ssk, K2tog [2 sts].

Thread yarn through rem sts and fasten.

Ears (make two)

Using dark brown yarn, cast on 2 sts and knit 1 row.

Next row: (Kfb) twice [4 sts].

Knit 1 row.

Next row: K1, (Kfb) twice, K1 [6 sts].
Knit 1 row.
Cast off all sts.

Eye markings (make two)
Using dark brown yarn, cast on 3 sts and work
2 rows in SS.
Cast off.

Nose
Using dark brown yarn, cast on 3 sts and work
2 rows in SS.
Next row: sl1, K2tog, psso. Fasten off rem st.

Making up
Sew back seam of body and stuff. Insert two 2.5cm
(1in) diameter coins before sewing the base in place.
Run a length of yarn through cast-on sts of head,
draw up and fasten. Sew seam of head. This will be
underneath when you have finished.
Stuff and sew back of head together.

Sew ears to head, making sure they have a 'rounded'
shape. Run a length of yarn around the outside edge
of the ear if necessary. Using the picture as a guide for
placement, sew on ears and nose, placing the cast-
on edge of the nose at the top and the decreased end
at the bottom.

Sew on the eye patches, rounding off the corners as
you sew them on. Using black sewing cotton and a
sewing needle, sew a bead to the centre of each eye
patch and pull the thread between the eyes to give
definition.

Sew head to body.

Sew arms together and stuff, inserting a short piece of
chenille stick if required. Attach arms to body.

Sew lower leg seam together, stuff and attach upper
leg to body, stuffing gently to give definition. Use the
picture as a guide to placing the legs before you sew
them on.

Sew tail seam, placing a chenille stick inside before
sewing up. Stuff wider end of tail slightly.

Sew tail to body.

It's après-ski for me ...

Skier-kat

Materials
Pale blue 4-ply (fingering) yarn
Cream kid mohair yarn (used double throughout)
Grey 4-ply (fingering) yarn
Silver lurex 4-ply (fingering) yarn
Two lolly sticks
Fine wire

Needles
2.75mm (UK 12, US 2) knitting needles
2.5mm (US 1/C) crochet hook (optional)

14

Instructions

Make adult meerkat (see pages 10–13).
**Remember to use cream kid mohair yarn
double throughout.**

Sweater (back)

Cast on 12 sts in pale blue yarn and work 8 rows in SS.
**Cast on 4 sts at beg of next two rows [20 sts].
Change to cream yarn and work 2 rows in SS.
Change to pale blue and knit 1 row.
Next row: (P1 pale blue, P1 cream) to end of row.
Knit 1 row in pale blue.
Knit 2 rows in cream.
Next row: (K1, P1) to end of row.
Work in K1, P1 rib for a further two rows. Cast off.

Sweater (front)

For right shoulder, cast on 4 sts using pale blue yarn and,
starting with a purl row, work 3 rows in SS. Cast on 2 sts at
the end of the next row.
Place sts on a length of yarn or spare needle.
For left shoulder, cast on 4 sts using pale blue yarn and
work 3 rows in SS.
Next row: join shoulders by purling across all sts for left
and right shoulders, placing extra cast-on sts in the middle.
Work 4 rows in SS.
Work as for sweater back from **.
Join right shoulder seam of sweater. Pick up and knit 10
sts across front of neck and 6 sts across back of neck and
work 6 rows in K1, P1 rib. Cast off.

Sleeves (make two)

Using pale blue yarn, cast on 14 sts and work 5 rows
in SS.
Change to cream and
work 2 rows in SS.
Change to pale blue
and work 2 rows
in SS.
Work 3 rows in K1,
P1 rib, as for
sweater back.
Cast off.

Hat

Using pale blue yarn, cast on 36 sts and work in K1, P1 rib for 8 rows.
Work 3 rows in SS. Change to cream and work 2 rows.
Change to pale blue and work 2 rows.
Next row: (P1, P2tog) to end of row [24 sts].
Knit 1 row.
Next row: P2tog to end of row [12 sts].
Thread yarn through rem sts and fasten, using this yarn to sew side seam of hat.

Skis (make two)

Cut a small piece of card the same width as the lolly stick and about 3cm (1¼in) long. Use sticky tape to fix it to the front of the lolly stick. Bend up slightly, using the picture as guidance. Using grey yarn, cast on 8 sts and work in SS until the work is long enough to fit along length of lolly stick. Thread yarn through sts and pull tight. Sew the knitting together underneath the ski, placing the cast-off edge at the front of the ski.

To make the foot loop, cast on 4 sts and work in GS until strip is long enough to fit over the foot from one edge of the ski to the other. Stitch to each side of the ski, placing loop towards back of ski and using the picture as guidance. Rep for the second ski.

Ski poles (make two)

Cut a length of wire to the right length for your meerkat and wrap silver yarn around the wire. Crochet the bottom of the pole as follows:
Using silver yarn, make 5ch and join with a sl st into first ch. 3ch (counts as 1*US*dc/*UK*tr), work 11*US*dc/*UK*tr into centre of circle, sl st into top of 3rd ch, fasten off. Alternatively, knit a circle as for the centre of Musical Meerkat's guitar (see page 73). Insert ski pole into centre of circle and fix approx 1cm (½in) up from end.

Making up

Join left shoulder seam of sweater. Sew cast-on edge of sleeve into armhole. Repeat for second sleeve. Fit sweater on to meerkat and sew sleeves and sides together, matching stripes. Sew collar seam and fold over using the picture as guidance. Fold up ribbed edge of hat and place on meerkat. Tack in place if necessary. Make a small pompom using cream yarn and sew to top of hat. Sew ski poles to hands. Slide feet into skis and tack to keep in place if necessary.

Beach Babe

Materials
Fuschia pink 4-ply (fingering) yarn
Purple 4-ply (fingering) yarn
Gold wire
Beads
Small amount of beige lace-weight yarn (used double throughout)
White 4-ply (fingering) linen yarn

Needles
2.75mm (UK 12, US 2) knitting needles
2.5mm (US 1/C) crochet hook (optional)

Instructions

Make adult meerkat (see pages 10–13).

Remember to use beige lace-weight yarn double throughout.

Bikini bottoms

Using pink yarn, cast on 16 sts and work 2 rows in SS.
Next row: K1, K2tog, knit to last 3 sts, ssk, K1 [14 sts].
Work 3 rows in SS.
Rep these 4 rows once more [12 sts].
Next row: (K1, K2tog) twice, yrn twice, (ssk, K1) twice [10 sts].
Next row: P4, Pfb into loop, P4 [10 sts].
Next row: K1, K2tog, knit to last 3 sts, ssk, K1 [8 sts].
Work 13 rows in SS.
Next row: K1, M1, knit to last st, M1, K1 [10 sts].
Work 3 rows in SS.
Rep the last 4 rows twice more [14 sts].
Cast off.
Crochet around bikini bottoms in purple yarn as follows:
*US*sc/*UK*dc into every other st around bikini bottoms. To make side ties, ch 14 sts.
Put bikini bottoms on the meerkat and sew side ties into a bow.
If you don't crochet, use a darning needle and purple yarn to embroider around the bikini using blanket stitch.

Bikini top (make two)

Using pink yarn, cast on 8 sts and work 2 rows in SS.
Next row: K3, K2tog, K3 [7 sts].
Purl 1 row.
Next row: K2, sl1, K2tog, psso, K2 [5 sts].
Purl 1 row.
Next row: K1, sl1, K2tog, psso, K1 [3 sts].
Purl 1 row.
Next row: sl1, K2tog, psso [1 st].
Thread yarn through rem st and fasten off.
Crochet around each side of bikini top, making shoulder straps with ch sts and joining the top in the centre. To make ties, ch 20 sts. Put top on and sew ties into a bow at the back. Thread some beads on to a length of yarn and sew to front of bikini, using the picture for guidance.

Tummy button

Using a double strand of beige lace-weight yarn, cast on 1 st.
Next row: knit into front, back and front of the st [3 sts].
Work 3 rows in SS.
Next row: sl1, K2tog, psso.
Fasten off rem st.
Sew tummy button into a bobble and attach to meerkat's tummy.

Bag

Cast on 10 sts in white linen yarn and work 8cm (3¼in) in GS. Cast off.

To make the handle, cast on 2 sts and work in GS until handle measures 8cm (3¼in). Fold bag in half and sew side seams. Attach handle as shown in the picture.

To make the flower centre, make a bobble in purple yarn as for tummy button.

To make the petals, cast on 4 sts, work 2 rows in GS. *Cast off 3 sts, knit 1 row. Cast on 3 sts, work 2 rows in GS.* Rep from * to * to make five petals in total. Cast off rem st. Thread a length of yarn through the inside edge of the petals and gather to form a flower shape. Attach to the bag and sew the bobble in the centre of the flower.

Earrings and tummy-button ring

Thread some beads on to a small amount of gold wire, bend into a circle and thread through the meerkats ears or tummy button. Snip the ends off carefully with scissors or wire cutters and ensure the ends are secured.

Prima Ballerina

Materials
Pale pink 4-ply (fingering) yarn
Pale pink lace-weight yarn
  (used double throughout)
Small amount of fine ribbon
Bead trim
Pale pink sewing cotton
Sewing needle

Needles
2.75mm (UK 12, US 2)
  knitting needles

Instructions

Make adult meerkat (see pages 10–13).

Remember to use pale pink lace-weight yarn double throughout.

Leotard (front)

Using pale pink 4-ply (fingering) yarn, cast on 10 sts and work 4 rows in SS.

Next row: K1, M1, knit to last st, M1, K1 [12 sts].

Work 3 rows in SS.

Rep last 4 rows a further 3 times [18 sts].

Cast on 2 sts at beg of next 2 rows [22 sts].

Work 2 rows in SS.

Next row: K1, K2tog, knit to last 3 sts, ssk, K1 [20 sts].

Purl 1 row.

Rep last 2 rows a further 5 times [10 sts].

Next row: cast off 2 sts at beg of next 2 rows [6 sts].

Work 2 rows in SS.

Next row: K2, cast off 2 sts, knit to end of row.

Working over first 2 sts, continue in SS until shoulder strap is long enough to sew to back of leotard. Cast off. Rejoin yarn to rem 2 sts and work to match other side.

Leotard (back)

Using pale pink 4-ply (fingering) yarn, cast on 10 sts and work 4 rows in SS.

Next row: K1, M1, knit to last st, M1, K1 [12 sts].

Purl 1 row.

The next 2 rows form a 'buttonhole' for the meerkat's tail.

Next row: K4, K2tog, yrn twice, ssk, knit to end of row.

Next row: P5, Pfb of loop, purl to end of row.

Next row: K1, M1, knit to last st, M1, K1 [14 sts].

Purl 1 row.

Rep last 2 rows twice more [18 sts].

Cast on 2 sts at beg of next 2 rows [22 sts].

Work 2 rows in SS.

Next row: K1, K2tog, knit to last 3 sts, ssk, K1 [20 sts].

Purl 1 row.

Rep last 2 rows a further 4 times [12 sts].

Work 2 rows in SS.

Next row: cast off 3 sts at beg of next 2 rows [6 sts].
Cast off rem 6 sts.

Tutu

Using pale pink lace-weight yarn, cast on 35 sts and purl 1 row.
Next row: (K1, M1) rep to last st, K1 [69 sts].
Purl 1 row.
Next row: (K1, M1) rep to last st, K1 [137 sts].
Purl 1 row.
Next row: (K1, M1) rep to last st, K1 [273 sts].
Purl 1 row.
Next row: (K1, M1) rep to last st, K1 [545 sts].
Purl 1 row.
Cast off loosely.

Ballet shoes (make two)

Using pale pink 4-ply (fingering) yarn, cast on 5 sts and work 12 rows in SS. Cast off.

Head band

Using pale pink 4-ply (fingering) yarn, cast on 2 sts and work 14 rows in SS. Cast off.

Making up

Sew bottom seam of leotard. Sew side seams, fitting to meerkat as you sew.

Attach shoulder straps to back of leotard. Sew bead trim around neckline, sewing one stitch between each bead.

Join side seam of tutu together and sew cast-on edge to leotard.

For each ballet shoe, fold cast-on end of shoe not quite in half (leave a small amount for sole of shoe) and sew to meerkat's foot. Sew a length of ribbon around shoe using pale pink sewing thread and a sewing needle, and sew the ribbon into a bow at back of leg, using the picture for guidance.

Sew headband to top of meerkat's head, curving it slightly. Sew bead trim to head band, as for tutu, making a loop in the middle.

Sew a ribbon bow on to the end of the tail.

Quack! Quack!

Fluffy Flippers

Materials
White 4-ply (fingering) yarn
Pale blue 4-ply (fingering) yarn
Yellow 4-ply (fingering) yarn
Orange 4-ply (fingering) yarn
Small amount of black
    embroidery thread
Toy filling

Needles
2.75mm (UK 12, US 2)
    knitting needles

Instructions

Make adult meerkat (see pages 10–13).

Swimsuit

Follow instructions for ballerina's leotard (page 24) but knit in stripes of 2 rows white followed by 2 rows pale blue.

Rubber ring

Using yellow yarn, cast on 14 sts.
*Work 4 rows in SS.
Next row: (RS): K10, w&t.
Next row: P6, w&t.
Next row: knit to end of row.
Purl 1 row.*
Rep from * to * until ring is long enough to fit over the meerkat's head and arms. Cast off.

Duck's head

Using yellow yarn, cast on 8 sts and work 2 rows in SS.
*Next row: K1, M1, knit to last st, M1, K1 [10 sts].
Purl 1 row.
Rep last 2 rows once more [12 sts].
Next row: K2tog, knit to last 3 sts, ssk, K1 [10 sts].
Purl 1 row.
Rep these 2 rows once more [8 sts].*
Rep from * to * for other side of head.
Cast off.

Duck's beak

Using orange yarn, cast on 4 sts and work 4 rows in GS.
Next row: K1, K2tog, K1 [3 sts].
Knit 1 row.
Cast off.

Duck's tail

Using yellow yarn, cast on 4 sts and work 2 rows in SS.
Next row: K1, M1, knit to last st, M1, K1 [6 sts].
Purl 1 row.
Rep these 2 rows once more [8 sts].
Next row: K1, K2tog, knit to last 3 sts, ssk, K1 [6 sts].
Purl 1 row.
Rep last 2 rows once more [4 sts].
Work 2 rows in SS and cast off.

Let's go for a swim!

Flippers (make two)

Using orange yarn, cast on 4 sts and work 2 rows in GS.

Next row: K1, M1, knit to last st, M1, K1 [6 sts].

Work 9 rows in GS.

Next row: K1, M1, knit to last st, M1, K1 [8 sts].

Knit 2 rows.

Rep last 3 rows twice more [12 sts].

Work 10 rows in GS.

Next row: K2tog at each end of row [10 sts]. Cast off.

To make straps for flippers, cast on 4 sts and work 12 rows in GS. Cast off.

Making up

Sew swimsuit together as for ballerina's leotard (page 25). Sew inside edge of rubber ring, stuffing as you go. Sew cast-on and cast-off ends together.

Sew front and back seams of duck's head, stuffing gently, and attach to front of rubber ring. Sew beak in place and embroider eyes, using picture for guidance. Sew seams on duck's tail, stuff and attach to back of ring.

Sew straps on to flippers.

Baby Meerkat

Materials
Beige and dark brown lace-weight yarn
  (used double throughout)
White 4-ply (fingering) yarn
Two black beads
Toy filling
Chenille stick
Miniature safety pin
Black sewing cotton
Sewing needle

For the teddy:
Orange 4-ply (fingering) yarn
Black sewing cotton
Small amount of toy filling
Sewing needle

Needles
2.75mm (UK 12, US 2) knitting needles

Instructions

Remember to use beige and dark brown lace-weight yarn double throughout.

Body

Using beige yarn, cast on 6 sts and work 2 rows in SS.

Next row: K3, M1, K3 [7 sts].

Purl 1 row.

Next row: K3, M1, K1, M1, K3 [9 sts].

Purl 1 row.

Next row: K3, M1, K3, M1, K3 [11 sts].

Purl 1 row.**

Next row: K3, M1, K5, M1, K3 [13 sts].

Work 3 rows in SS.

Next row: K3, M1, K7, M1, K3 [15 sts].

Work 3 rows in SS.

Next row: K2, (K2tog, K1) 3 times, K2tog, K2 [11 sts].

Purl 1 row.

Next row: cast off 4 sts, Kfb, K1, cast off rem 4 sts [4 sts].

Rejoin yarn to rem sts and work 4 rows in SS.

Cast off.

Head

Using beige yarn, cast on 6 sts and work as for body to **.

Next row: K6, K2togtbl, K1, turn.

Next row: sl1, P2, P2tog, P1, turn.

Next row: sl1, K3, K2togtbl, K1 [8 sts].

Next row: P3, cast off 2 sts, P3.

Next row: K3, turn and cast off these 3 sts. Rejoin yarn to rem 3 sts, rep to match other side.

Arms (make two)

Using beige yarn, cast on 4 sts and work 6 rows in SS.

Thread yarn through sts and fasten.

Legs (make two)

Using beige yarn, cast on 4 sts and work 4 rows in SS. This forms the upper leg.

Next row: cast off 2 sts at beg of row.

Purl 1 row.

Next row: cast on 2 sts and work 2 rows in SS.

Cast off sts. This is the 'foot' end of the leg.

Tail

Using beige yarn, cast on 4 sts and work 8 rows in SS.

Next row: K1, K2tog, K1 [3 sts].

Purl 1 row.

Change to dark brown and work 2 rows in SS.

Thread yarn through rem sts and fasten.

Ears (make two)

Using dark brown yarn, cast on 3 sts and work 2 rows in GS.

Next row: sl1, K2tog, psso. Fasten rem st.

Making up

Sew seam of body from neck downwards. Stuff body and sew base into place.

Run a thread through the cast-on sts of the head and sew seam towards back of head. Stuff and sew seam at back of head.

Attach head to body.

Sew seams of arms, adding a small length of chenille stick if required. Sew to sides of body.

Fold over lower part of leg and sew sides together. Sew upper leg to body. Repeat for second leg, turning it the other way around before attaching to body.

Attach ears to head, using the picture as a guide.

Embroider nose and eye patches using dark brown yarn. With black sewing cotton and a sewing needle, sew a bead into the centre of each eye patch to make the eyes.

Sew tail seam and attach to base of body at the back.

Embroider tummy button using a double strand of beige lace-weight yarn.

Nappy

Using white yarn, cast on 8 sts and work 4 rows in GS.

Next row: K2tog at each end of row [6 sts].

Knit 1 row.

Rep last 2 rows once more [4 sts].
Work 4 rows in GS.
Next row: K1, M1, knit to last st, M1, K1 [6 sts].
Knit 1 row.
Rep last 2 rows once more [8 sts].
Work 3 rows in GS.
The next 2 rows form a hole for the tail to go through.
Next row: K2, K2tog, yrn twice, ssk, K2 [8 sts].
Next row: K3, Kfb of loop, K3 [8 sts].
Knit 1 row.
Cast on 6 sts at beg of next 2 rows [20 sts].
Work 3 rows in GS.
Cast off.
Thread tail through hole in nappy. Fold long edges to front of nappy and sew in place. Sew safety pin to front of nappy.

Teddy bear's head
Cast on 5 sts.
Next row: K2, M1, K1, M1, K2 [7 sts].
Purl 1 row.
Next row: K3, M1, K1, M1, K3 [9 sts].
Work 3 rows in SS.
Next row: K1, K2tog, K3, K2tog, K1 [7 sts].
Thread yarn through rem sts and tighten. Use this length of yarn to sew side seam of head.

Teddy bear's ears (make two)
Cast on 2 sts and knit 1 row.
Next row: K2tog.
Fasten off rem st.

Teddy bear's body
Cast on 8 sts.
Next row: K3, M1, K2, M1, K3 [10 sts].
Next row: P4, M1, P2, M1, P4 [12 sts].
Continue to inc in this way, either side of the 2 centre sts on every row, until you have 16 sts.
Work 2 rows in SS.
Next row: K1, (K2tog, K2) 3 times, K2tog, K1 [12 sts].
Purl 1 row.
Next row: K2tog, K1, (K2tog) 3 times, K1, K2tog, K1 [7 sts].
Purl 1 row, thread yarn through rem sts and tighten. Use length of yarn to sew side seam of body.

Teddy bear's arms (make two)
Cast on 4 sts and make an i-cord measuring 1.5cm (⅝in) (see page 94).
Thread yarn through sts and fasten.

Teddy bear's legs (make two)
Cast on 5 sts, K4 and turn.
Next row: K3 and turn.
Working only over centre 3 sts, work a further 5 rows in SS.
Next row: knit across 3 centre sts and last st.
Next row: purl across all sts.
Continue working an i-cord over all sts until work measures 2cm (¾in).

Making up
Sew side seam of head, stuffing gently with toy filling as you sew. Sew ears to head using picture as guidance. Embroider eyes, nose and mouth using embroidery thread.

Sew side seam of body, stuffing gently with toy filling as you sew. Sew arms to side of teddy, running the thread through from one arm to the other and back so the arms can move up and down.

For each leg, sew the gaps at the sides of the foot to the leg. Sew the legs to the body in the same way as the arms.

Please dance with me!

Flower Power

Materials
Fuschia pink 4-ply
   (fingering) yarn
Green lace-weight yarn
Fine wire

Needles
2.75mm (UK 12, US 2)
   knitting needles

Instructions

Make baby meerkat (see pages 30–33).

Underskirt and top

Using green yarn, cast on as follows:

(Cast on 5 sts, cast off 2 sts, sl resulting st back to LH needle) 11 times, cast on 2 sts. This row forms a picot edging [35 sts].

Work 4 rows in SS.

Next row: K1, (K1, K2tog) 11 times, K1 [24 sts].

Next row: (K2tog, K1) to end of row [16 sts].

Knit 3 rows.

Next row: (K2, K2tog) to end of row [12 sts].

Knit 3 rows.

Change to pink yarn and cast off loosely so that the top of the dress fits around the meerkat.

Petal overskirt (make six)

Using pink yarn, cast on 4 sts and work 2 rows in SS.

Next row: K2, M1, K2 [5 sts].

Work 3 rows in SS.

Next row: K2tog, K1, ssk [3 sts].

Purl 1 row.

sl1, K2tog, psso.

Fasten off rem st.

Flower hat

To make the flower centre, cast on 1 st using a double strand of green lace-weight yarn.

Next row: knit into front, back and front of the st [3 sts].

Work 3 rows in SS.

Next row: sl1, K2tog, psso.

Fasten off rem st.

To make the petals, cast on 4 sts using pink yarn.

Work 2 rows in GS.

*Cast off 3 sts, knit 1 row.

Cast on 3 sts, work 2 rows in GS.*

Rep from * to * to make five petals in total. Cast off rem st.

Wings

Using green yarn, cast on 3 sts.

Knit 1 row.

*Next row: K1, M1, K1, M1, K1 [5 sts].

Work 6 rows in GS.

Next row: K2tog, K1, K2tog [3 sts].

Knit 1 row.*

Rep from * to *. Cast off rem sts.

Making up

Sew seam of underskirt and fit to meerkat. Neatly stitch together the pink cast-off sts and use the rem yarn to make shoulder straps using the picture as guidance.

Sew ends of yarn in and lightly press petals. Stitch the top of the petals together and sew to underskirt, as shown.

Thread a length of yarn through the inside edge of the petals for the flower hat and gather to form a flower shape. Sew the flower to the top of the meerkat's head and sew the bobble in the centre.

Sew a length of fine wire around the edges of the wings and sew to back of dress.

The Count

Materials
Black 4-ply (fingering) yarn
Purple 4-ply (fingering) yarn
Small amount of white 4-ply
    (fingering) yarn
Small amount of fine
    black ribbon
Stitch marker

Needles
2.75mm (UK 12, US 2)
    knitting needles

That coffin sucks!

Lunchtime – fancy a bite?

Instructions

Make adult meerkat (see pages 10–13).

Cape (back)

Using black yarn, cast on 14 sts and work 3 rows in SS.

Next row: P6, PM, P2, PM, P6.

Next row: Knit to M, M1, SM, knit to next M, SM, M1, knit to end of row [16 sts].

Purl 1 row.

Rep the last 2 rows until you have 38 sts in total. Remove markers.

Work 5 rows in SS.

Next row: change to purple and purl to end of row.

Cast off in purple.

Cape (right front)

Using black yarn, cast on 8 sts and work 3 rows in SS.
Next row: P3, PM, P5.
Next row: knit to M, M1, SM, knit to end of row [9 sts].
Purl 1 row.
Rep last 2 rows until there are 20 sts.
Next row: K1, K2tog, knit to end of row.
Purl 1 row.
Rep last 2 rows 3 more times [16 sts], BUT on last row change to purple and purl to end of row.
Continue by picking up and purling 20 sts along front edge [36 sts].
Cast off in purple.

Cape (left front)

Using black yarn, cast on 8 sts and work 3 rows in SS.
Next row: P5, PM, P3.
Next row: knit to M, M1, SM, knit to end of row [9 sts].
Purl 1 row.
Rep last 2 rows until there are 20 sts. Remove marker.
Next row: knit to last 3 sts, ssk, K1.
Purl 1 row.
Rep last 2 rows 3 more times, but on last row leave sts on needle and change to purple yarn. Join yarn at top of front edge and pick up 20 sts purlwise along front edge and purl across sts on needle. Cast off.

Collar

Using black yarn, cast on 14 sts and work 2 rows in SS.
Next row: K1, M1, knit to last st, M1, K1 [16 sts].
Purl 1 row.
Rep last 2 rows a further 4 times until there are 24 sts.
Purl 1 row (RS).
Change to purple and purl 1 row. This row creates a fold line.
Next row: K1, K2tog, knit to last 3 sts, ssk, K1 [22 sts].
Purl 1 row.
Rep last 2 rows a further 5 times until 12 sts rem.
Cast off.

Teeth (make two)

Using white yarn, cast on 1 st and knit into it.
Next row: Kfbf [3 sts].
Purl 1 row.
Cast off.

Hair

Using black yarn, cast on 1 st.
Next row: Kfbf [3 sts].
Purl 1 row.
Next row: K1, M1, knit to last st, M1, K1 [5 sts].
Purl 1 row.
Rep these 2 rows once more [7 sts].
Cast on 3 sts at beg of next 2 rows [13 sts].
Cast off 3 sts at beg of next 2 rows [7 sts].
Cast on 4 sts at beg of next two rows [15 sts].
Next row: K5, K2tog, K1, ssk, knit to end of row [13 sts].
Rep this row working a dec either side of the centre st until 3 sts rem.
Sl1, K2tog, psso. Fasten off rem st.

Making up

Sew side and shoulder seams of cape. With wrong sides together, sew sloping edges of collar together. Stitch closed bottom edge of collar and sew to top of cape. Sew teeth to either side of nose, using the picture as guidance. Sew hair to head, placing the cast-on point in middle of forehead.

Santa Paws

Materials

Red 4-ply (fingering) yarn
White sparkly 4-ply (fingering) yarn
Cream lace-weight yarn (used
 double throughout)
Brown 4-ply (fingering) yarn
Black 4-ply (fingering) yarn
Three tiny black buttons
Small brass bell
Small amount of silver 4-ply
 (fingering) yarn
Small amount of toy filling
Black sewing cotton
Sewing needle

Needles

2.75mm (UK 12, US 2)
 knitting needles

For the pattern for the teddy, see page 33.

Instructions

Make adult meerkat (see pages 10–13).

Remember to use cream lace-weight yarn double throughout.

Jacket (back)

Using red yarn, cast on 12 sts and work 8 rows in SS.
Cast on 3 sts at beg of next 2 rows [18 sts].
Work 2 rows in SS.
Next row: K1, M1, knit to last st, M1, K1 [20 sts].
Work 3 rows in SS.
Rep last 4 rows once more [22 sts].
Work 2 rows in SS.
Change to white sparkly yarn and knit to end of row.
Next row (WS): starting with a knit row, work 5 rows in rev SS. Cast off.

Jacket (right front)

Using red yarn, cast on 4 sts and work 8 rows in SS.
Cast on 3 sts at the beg of the next row [7 sts].
Work 3 rows in SS.
Next row: K1, M1, K to end of row [8 sts].
Work 3 rows in SS.

Rep the last four rows once more [9 sts].
Work 2 rows in SS.
Change to white sparkly yarn and knit to end of row.
Next row (WS): Starting with a K row, work 5 rows in rev SS. Cast off.

Jacket (left front)

Using red yarn, cast on 4 sts and work 8 rows in SS.
Cast on 3 sts at end of next row [7 sts].
Work 3 rows in SS.
Next row: knit to last st, M1, K1 [8 sts].
Work 3 rows in SS.
Rep last 4 rows once more [9 sts].
Work 2 rows in SS.
Change to white sparkly yarn and knit to end of row.
Next row (WS): starting with a knit row, work 5 rows in rev SS. Cast off.
Using white sparkly yarn, pick up and knit approx. 20 sts along front edge of jacket. Work 4 rows in rev SS. Cast off.

Sleeves (make two)

Using red yarn, cast on 14 sts and work 8 rows in SS.
Change to white sparkly yarn and knit to end of row.
Starting with a knit row, work 5 rows in rev SS.
Cast off.

Collar

Using white sparkly yarn, cast on 6 sts and knit 1 row.
Next row: K2tog at beg of row [5 sts].
Knit 4 rows.
Rep last 5 rows once more [4 sts].
Knit 10 rows.
Next row: Kfb at beg of row.
Knit 4 rows.
Next row: Kfb at beg of row [5 sts].
Knit 1 row. Cast off.

Hat

Using white sparkly yarn, cast on 28 sts and work 5 rows in rev SS.
Change to red yarn.
Work 8 rows in SS.
Next row: (K1, K2tog) 9 times, K1 [19 sts].
Purl 1 row.
Next row: (K1, K2tog) 6 times, K1 [13 sts].
Work 3 rows in SS.
Next row: K2tog to last st, K1 [7 sts].
Purl 1 row.

Thread yarn through rem sts. Sew up side seam of hat, folding the top over slightly as shown in the picture. Sew bell to top of hat.

Beard
Using cream yarn, cast on 5 sts and knit 2 rows.
Next row: K1, M1, knit to last st, M1, K1 [7 sts].
Knit 2 rows.
Rep last 3 rows once more [9 sts].
Knit 4 rows.
Cast on 3 sts at beg of next 2 rows [15 sts].
Cast off.

Moustache
Using cream yarn, cast on 5 sts and knit 1 row.
Cast off 2 sts at beg of next 2 rows.
Fasten off rem st.

Eyebrows
Using cream yarn, cast on 3 sts. Cast off.

Sack
Using brown yarn, cast on 7 sts and work 8 rows in SS.
Cast on 10 sts at beg of next 2 rows [27 sts].
Work 24 rows in SS. Cast off.

Belt
Using black yarn, cast on 3 sts and work in GS until the belt fits around the jacket.

Making up
Sew shoulder seams together. Sew side seams of the jacket and sleeves. Sew sleeves on to jacket and place on meerkat. Sew front seam closed. Sew bottom edge of jacket to meerkat. Sew collar to jacket. Sew belt around middle of jacket and embroider buckle using silver thread. Sew on buttons using black sewing cotton.

Sew hat on to meerkat's head. Sew on beard, eyebrows and moustache, using picture as a guide.

Sew side seam of sack and fold up base. Sew base in place. Use a length of yarn to tie around the top of the sack.

Ho Ho Ho!

Are we nearly there yet?

Meerkat Clan

Materials
Pink 4-ply (fingering) yarn
Pale blue 4-ply (fingering) yarn
Three tiny buttons
Small amount of pink ribbon
Pale pink sewing cotton
Sewing needle

Needles
2.75mm (UK 12, US 2)
   knitting needles
2.5mm (US 1/C) crochet
   hook (optional)

Instructions

Make adult meerkat (see pages 10–13) and two baby meerkats (pages 30–33).

Baby sling

Using pale blue yarn, cast on 69 sts and work 2 rows in GS.

Next row: cast off 32 sts, K4 (5 sts on RH needle), cast off 32 sts.

With RS facing, rejoin yarn to rem 5 sts and work 2 rows in GS.

Next row: K1, M1, knit to last st, M1, K1 [7 sts].

Knit 1 row.

Rep last 2 rows once more [9 sts].

Cast on 6 sts at beg of next 2 rows [21 sts].

Work 5 rows in GS.

Next row: cast off 8 sts at beg of next 2 rows [5 sts].

Work 2 rows in GS.

Next row: K2tog at each end of next row [3 sts].

Work 7 rows in GS.

Cast off rem sts.

Making up

Sew seam at back of sling and sew gusset to bottom of this seam. Cross the ties over the mother meerkat's back and sew on to the baby sling using the picture as guidance. Sew buttons on to the baby sling where the ties attach.

Toddler dress (front)

Cast on as follows in pink yarn:

(Cast on 4 sts, cast off 2 sts, sl resulting st back to LH needle) 7 times, cast on 1 st. This row forms the picot edging [15 sts].

Work 2 rows in GS.

Work 2 rows in SS.

*Next row: K1, K2tog, knit to last 3 sts, ssk, K1 [13 sts].

Purl 1 row.*

Rep last 2 rows from * to * until 7 sts rem.**

Cast off 2 sts at beg of next 2 rows.

Cast off rem 3 sts.

Toddler dress (back)

Work as for front to **.

Cast off all sts.

Making up

Sew side seams of dress. Make a shoulder strap by crocheting a chain from one side of the dress top to the back. Repeat to make second shoulder strap on the other side. If you do not crochet you can sew short lengths of yarn in place to make shoulder straps. Sew button to front of dress. Make a ribbon bow and sew to top of toddler's ear using pink sewing cotton.

I am a superstar!

Bollywood

Materials
Fuschia pink lace-weight yarn
Small amount of gold lurex 4-ply
    (fingering) yarn
Glass beads
Sewing needle
Stitch marker

Needles
2.75mm (UK 12, US 2)
    knitting needles

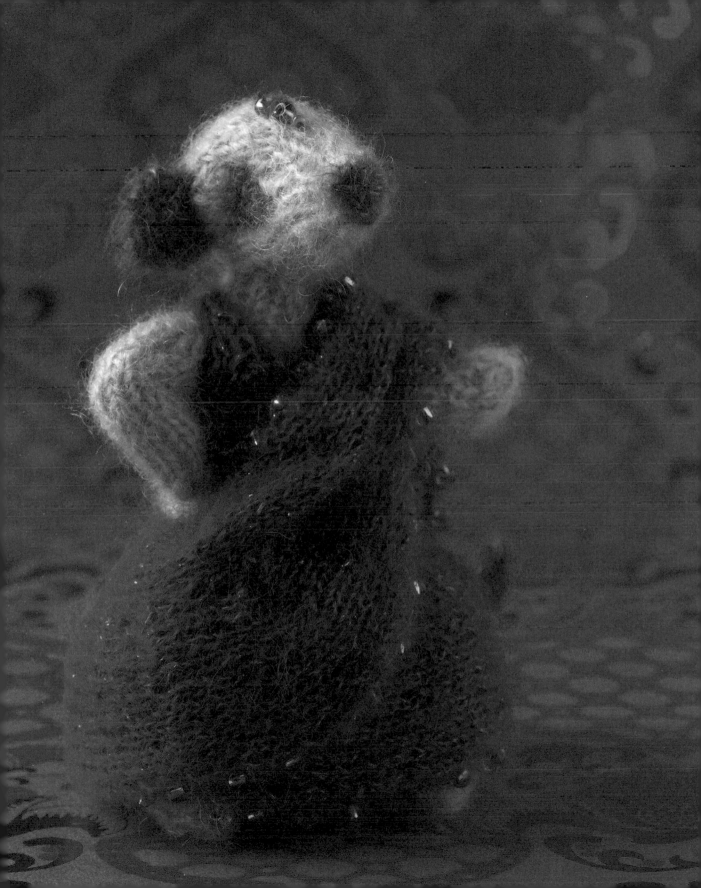

Instructions

Make adult meerkat (see pages 10–13).

Top (front)

*Using a gold lurex yarn, cast on 12 sts.
Change to a double strand of fuschia pink yarn and work 2 rows in SS.
Next row: K1, K2tog, knit to last 3 sts, ssk, K1.
Purl 1 row.
Rep last 2 rows once more [8 sts].*
Next row: K2, K2tog, turn and continue on rem 3 sts.
Work 3 rows in SS.
Next row: K1, K2tog [2 sts].
Work 2 rows in SS and cast off rem 2 sts.
With RS facing, rejoin yarn to rem 4 sts.
Next row: ssk, K2 [3 sts].
Work 3 rows in SS.
Next row: ssk, K1 [2 sts].
Work 2 rows in SS and cast off rem 2 sts.

Top (back)

Work as for front from * to *.
Next row: K1, K2tog, knit to last 3 sts, ssk, K1 [6 sts].
Work 5 rows in SS and cast off rem 6 sts.

Sari

Cast on 18 sts.
*Work 4 rows in SS.
Next row: K10, w&t.
Next row: P10, turn.*
Rep from * to * until sari is long enough to fit around the meerkat and overlap slightly.
Next row: K10, w&t.
Next row: P10, turn.
Rep these 2 'short rows' twice more to make more shaping. Place marker at waist edge.
Next row: knit across all sts, knitting the 'wraps' together as you go to make them less noticeable.
Work 3 rows in SS.
Next row: K1, K2tog, knit to end of row [17 sts].
Work 3 rows in SS.
Rep last 4 rows a further 7 times until you have 10 sts.
Work in SS until this strip of sari is long enough to go over the meerkat's shoulder and reach down her back, using the picture for guidance.
Cast off.

Making up

Sew one side seam and shoulder seam of top and fit to meerkat. Sew second shoulder and side seam.

Using a length of fuschia pink lace-weight yarn and a sewing needle, sew beads around the bottom edge of the sari, along the end and straight length that will be over the meerkat's shoulder.

Place sari edge with marker on waist and sew in place starting at right side and working across the front, and around the back to starting point. Remove marker and finish off. Using picture as a guide, drape remaining sari over left shoulder and down the back. Pleat and sew the sari in place at the shoulder.

Using fuschia pink yarn, embroider a French knot in the middle of the meerkat's forehead and sew beads above and below to make the bindi decoration.

Bollywood or bust!

Soccer Star

Materials
White 4-ply (fingering) yarn
Red 4-ply (fingering) yarn
Black 4-ply (fingering) yarn
Toy filling

Needles
2.75mm (UK 12, US 2)
   knitting needles

He shoots!
He scores!

Instructions

Make adult meerkat (see pages 10–13).

Football shirt (back)

The shirt is worked sideways from sleeve to sleeve.
Using red yarn, cast on 12 sts and work 4 rows in SS.
Change to white and knit 1 row.
Next row: cast on 5 sts and purl 1 row [17 sts].
Work 2 rows in white and change to red.
Work 4 rows in red.
Work another 11 rows, changing colour every 4 rows.
Next row (WS): cast off 5 sts, purl to end of row [12 sts].
Change to red and work 4 rows. Cast off.

Football shirt (front)

Using white yarn, cast on 12 sts and work 4 rows in SS.
Change to red and knit 1 row.
Next row: cast on 5 sts and purl 1 row [17 sts].
Work 2 rows in red.
Change to white and knit 1 row.
Cast off 2 sts at beg of next row [15 sts].
Knit 1 row.
Cast off 1 st at beg of next row [14 sts].
Change to red and work 4 rows.
Change to white and knit 1 row.
Cast on 1 st at beg of next row [15 sts].
Knit 1 row.
Cast on 2 sts at beg of next row [17 sts].
Change to red and work 3 rows.
Cast off 5 sts, purl to end of row [12 sts].
Change to white and work 4 rows. Cast off.

Sleeves (make two)

Using red yarn, cast on 14 sts and work
4 rows in SS.
Change to white and work 2 rows in GS.
Cast off.

Football

Using white yarn, cast on 14 sts and purl 1 row.
Work increase rows as follows:
K1, (Kfb, K1, Kfb) to last st, K1 [22 sts].
Purl 1 row.
K1, (Kfb, K3, Kfb) to last st, K1 [30 sts].
Purl 1 row.
Work 4 rows in SS.
Work decrease rows as follows:
K1, (K2tog, K3, ssk) to last st, K1 [22 sts].
Purl 1 row.

K1, (K2tog, K1, ssk) to last st, K1 [14 sts].
Purl 1 row.
Thread yarn through rem sts and fasten off.
To make the black patches for the football:
Using black yarn, cast on 3 sts and work 3 rows in SS. Cast off.
Make seven patches altogether.

Making up
Join one shoulder seam of football shirt. With RS facing, pick up and knit 7 sts across back of neck and 10 sts across front neck.
Knit 1 row. Cast off.
Join one side seam and, with RS facing, pick up and knit 20 sts along bottom edge.
Knit 1 row. Cast off.
Put the football shirt on the meerkat and join the second shoulder seam and side seam.
Sew seam of football, stuff with toy filling and sew black patches on to football using the picture as guidance.
Embroider the number on the back of the football shirt using backstitch.

Acrobat Kats

Materials
White 4-ply (fingering) yarn
Small amount of red and
    blue 4-ply (fingering) yarn

Needles
2.75mm (UK 12, US 2)
    knitting needles

Instructions

Make 3 adult meerkats (or as many as you want) (see pages 10–13).

Leotard (front)

Using white yarn, cast on 10 sts and work 4 rows in SS.

Next row: K1, M1, knit to last st, M1, K1 [12 sts].

Work 3 rows in SS.

Rep last 4 rows a further 3 times until you have 18 sts.

Cast on 2 sts at beg of next 2 rows [22 sts].

Work 2 rows in SS.

*Change to blue yarn.

Next row: K1, K2tog, knit to last 3 sts, ssk, K1 [20 sts].

Purl 1 row.

Rep last 2 rows once more [18 sts].

Change to white yarn.

Next row: K1, K2tog, knit to last 3 sts, ssk, K1 [16 sts].

Purl 1 row.

Change to red yarn.

Next row: K1, K2tog, knit to last 3 sts, ssk, K1 [14 sts].

Purl 1 row.

Rep last 2 rows once more [12 sts].

Change to white yarn.*

Next row: K1, K2tog, knit to last 3 sts, ssk, K1 [10 sts].

Purl 1 row.

Next row: cast off 2 sts at beg of next 2 rows [6 sts].

Work 2 rows in SS.

Next row: K2, cast off 2 sts, knit to end of row.

Working over first 2 sts, continue in SS until shoulder strap is long enough to sew to back of leotard. Cast off.

Rejoin yarn to second shoulder strap and work to match other side.

Leotard (back)

Using white yarn, cast on 10 sts and work 4 rows in SS.

Next row: K1, M1, knit to last st, M1, K1 [12 sts].

Purl 1 row.

The next 2 rows form a 'buttonhole' for the meerkat's tail.

Next row: K4, K2tog, yrn twice, ssk, K4 [12 sts].

Next row: P5, Pfb of loop, P5 [12 sts].

Next row: K1, M1, knit to last st, M1, K1 [14 sts].

Purl 1 row.

Rep last 2 rows twice more until you have 18 sts.

Cast on 2 sts at beg of next 2 rows [22 sts].

Work 2 rows in SS.

Work as for front from * to *.

Work 2 rows in SS [12 sts].

Next row: cast off 3 sts at beg of next 2 rows [6 sts].

Cast off rem 6 sts.

Making up

Sew bottom seam of leotard. Sew side seams, fitting to meerkat as you sew.

Attach shoulder straps to back of leotard, crossing the straps over at the back.

Yippee! I passed!

School for Kats

Materials
White 4-ply (fingering) yarn
Black 4-ply (fingering) yarn
Small amount of fine red ribbon
Stitch marker

Needles
2.75mm (UK 12, US 2)
   knitting needles

Instructions

Make adult meerkat (see pages 10–13).

Gown (back)

Using black yarn, cast on 12 sts and work 8 rows in SS.

Cast on 2 sts at beg of next 2 rows [16 sts].

Knit 1 row.

Next row: P7, PM, P2, PM, P7.

Next row: knit to M, M1, SM, knit to next M, SM, M1, knit to end of row [18 sts].

Purl 1 row.

Rep last 2 rows a further 10 times until you have 38 sts in total.

Work 6 rows in SS. Cast off.

Gown (right front)

Using black yarn, cast on 3 sts and work 2 rows in SS.

Cast on 1 st at end of next row [4 sts].

Knit 1 row.

Cast on 2 sts at end of next row [6 sts].

Work 2 rows in SS.

Cast on 2 sts at end of next row [8 sts].

Knit 1 row.

Next row: P5, PM, P3.

Next row: knit to M, SM, M1, knit to end of row [9 sts].

Purl 1 row.

Rep last 2 rows a further 10 times until there are 19 sts.

Work 6 rows in SS. Cast off.

Gown (left front)

Using black yarn, cast on 3 sts and work 2 rows in SS.

Cast on 1 st at beg of next row [4 sts].

Purl 1 row.

Cast on 2 sts at beg of next row [6 sts].

Work 2 rows in SS.

Cast on 2 sts at beg of next row [8 sts].

Knit 1 row.

Next row: P3, PM, P5.

Next row: knit to M, M1, SM, knit to end of row [9 sts].

Purl 1 row.

Rep last 2 rows a further 10 times until there are 19 sts.

Work 6 rows in SS. Cast off.

Sleeves (make two)

Using black yarn, cast on 14 sts and work 6 rows in SS.

Next row: K1, M1, knit to last st, M1, K1 [16 sts].

Purl 1 row.
Rep last 2 rows twice more [20 sts].
Work 2 rows in SS. Cast off.

Collar

Using white yarn, cast on 1 st.
Kfbf [3 sts].
Purl 1 row.
Next row: K1, M1, knit to last st, M1, K1 [5 sts].
Purl 1 row.
Rep last 2 rows a further 6 times until there are 17 sts.
Next row: K4, cast off 9 sts, knit to end of row.
Turn and, working over the first 4 sts, work 9 rows in SS.
Next row: K2tog, knit to end of row (dec worked at outside edge) [3 sts].
Purl 1 row.
Rep last 2 rows twice more and cast off rem st.
With WS facing, rejoin yarn to rem 4 sts and work
9 rows in SS.
Next row: K2, ssk (dec worked at outside edge) [3 sts].
Purl 1 row.
Rep last 2 rows twice more and cast off rem st.

Hat

For orown of hat, use black yarn and
cast on 14 sts. Work 4 rows in SS.
Next row: (K2tog) to end of row [7 sts].
Thread yarn through rem sts and fasten off.
For top of hat, use black yarn and cast on
12 sts. Work in GS until the piece is square.
Cast off. Make a small tassel by plaiting 3
strands of yarn, tying in a knot and leaving
approximately 1.5cm (¾in) of yarn below the
knot. Attach to one corner of the hat.

Scroll

Using white yarn, cast on 14 sts and work
16 rows in SS. Cast off. Allow the knitting to
roll up with WS facing outwards.

Making up

Sew side and shoulder seams of gown. Sew
in sleeves and place on meerkat. Sew sloped
edges of collar together and stitch to gown with
the point at the back, just above waist level.
Sew top of hat to centre of crown and sew crown
to meerkat's head, with the tassel at the back.
Tie a small amount of red ribbon around the scroll
and sew to meerkat's arms.

Meer Punk

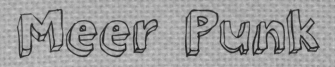
This pin is pinching my nose!

Instructions

Make adult meerkat (see pages 10–13).

Jacket (back)

Using black yarn, cast on 12 sts and work 8 rows in SS.

Cast on 4 sts at beg of next 2 rows [20 sts].

Work 8 rows in SS.

Work 4 rows in GS.

Cast off.

Jacket (right front)

Using black yarn, cast on 4 sts and work 8 rows in SS.

Cast on 4 sts at beg of next row.

Work 9 rows in SS.

Work 4 rows in GS.

Cast off.

Jacket (left front)

Using black yarn, cast on 4 sts and work 8 rows in SS.

Cast on 4 sts at end of next row (WS).

Work 9 rows in SS.

Work 4 rows in GS.

Cast off.

Sleeves

Using black yarn, cast on 14 sts and work 8 rows in SS.

Work 4 rows in GS.

Cast off.

Collar (make two)

Using black yarn, cast on 2 sts and knit 2 rows.

Next row: K1, M1, knit to end of row [3 sts].

Knit 1 row.

Rep last 2 rows twice more [5 sts].

Knit 2 rows.

Cast off 3 sts at beg of next row [2 sts].

Knit 1 row.

Cast on 3 sts at beg of foll row [5 sts].

Knit 1 row.

Next row: K1, K2tog, knit to end of row [4 sts].

Knit 1 row.

Rep last 2 rows once more [3 sts].

Continue to work in GS over rem 3 sts until collar is long enough to reach to centre back of neck.

T-shirt (just showing under jacket)

Using neon green yarn, cast on 6 sts and work 2 rows in GS.
Work 10 rows in SS. Cast off.

Making up

Sew T-shirt to front of meerkat with GS rows at neck edge.

Sew shoulder seams and side seams of jacket together and place on meerkat. Sew collar around neck and down each front, joining the seam at the back of the neck. Sew in place so that it stands up slightly. Sew centre front of jacket together from bottom to start of collar. For each sleeve, sew side seam and sew into armholes.

Attach safety pins and lengths of chain.

Hair

Using the picture as a guide, take a double strand of green lace-weight yarn and a crochet hook or needle, thread two double strands of yarn through a st in centre of head, and pull ends of yarn through loop to secure. Continue down back of head to create a Mohican hairstyle. Trim and shape for effect.

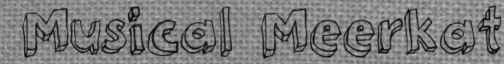

Musical Meerkat

Materials
Denim blue 4-ply (fingering) yarn
White 4-ply (fingering) yarn
Silver lurex 4-ply (fingering) yarn
Small gold beads
Orange embroidery thread
Gold and bronze embroidery thread
Small amount of black, grey, red and
    brown 4-ply (fingering) yarn
Toy filling
Chenille sticks

Needles
2.75mm (UK 12, US 2) knitting
    needles (double pointed
    recommended)

Instructions

Make adult meerkat (see pages 10–13).

Jacket (back)
Using blue yarn, cast on 12 sts and work 8 rows in SS.
Cast on 4 sts at beg of next 2 rows.
Work 8 rows in SS.
Work 4 rows in GS. Cast off.

Jacket (right front)
Using blue yarn, cast on 3 sts and work 3 rows in SS.
Cast on 2 sts at beg of next row (neck shaping) [5 sts].
Work 4 rows.
Cast on 3 sts at beg of next row (armhole shaping)
[8 sts].
Work 8 rows in SS.
Work 4 rows in GS. Cast off.

Jacket (left front)
Using blue yarn, cast on 3 sts and work 2 rows
in SS.
Cast on 3 sts at beg of next row (neck shaping) [5 sts].
Work 3 rows.
Cast on 3 sts at beg of next row (armhole shaping) [8 sts].
Work 9 rows in SS.
Cast on 2 sts at beg of next row and work 4 rows in GS.
Cast off.

Sleeves (make two)
Using blue yarn, cast on 15 sts and work 8 rows in SS.
Work 4 rows in GS. Cast off.

T-shirt (back)
Using white yarn, cast on 20 sts and work 6 rows in SS.
Cast off.

T-shirt (front)
Using white yarn, cast on 20 sts and work 6 rows in SS.
Cast off 7 sts at beg of next 2 rows [6 sts].
Work 10 rows in SS and then 4 rows in GS.
Cast off.

Making up the jacket and T-shirt
With RS facing, pick up approximately 9 sts along jacket right front down to extra cast-on sts. Knit 1 row and cast off.
With RS facing, pick up approximately 11 sts along jacket left front, knit 1 row and cast off.
Join shoulder seams and, with RS facing, pick up approximately 15 sts along length of neck. Knit 1 row and cast off. Sew side seams of jacket together. Sew sleeve seams and stitch to jacket body.

Template for
the guitar
(actual size)

Sew back of T-shirt to bottom of jacket and sew front of T-shirt inside open edges of jacket, matching and sewing side seams.

Using orange thread, embroider around the edges of the jacket in backstitch, using the picture for guidance. Embroider French knots in silver lurex to make the buttons on the front of the jacket and embroider one button on each sleeve edge.

Guitar body (make two)

Using red yarn, cast on 7 sts and work 2 rows in SS.
Next row: K1, M1, knit to last st, M1, K1 [9 sts].
Purl 1 row.
Rep last 2 rows once more [11 sts].
Work 2 rows in SS.
Next row: K1, K2tog, knit to last 3 sts, ssk, K1 [9 sts].
Purl 1 row.
Rep last 2 rows once more [7 sts].
Next row: K1, M1, knit to last st, M1, K1 [9 sts].
Purl 1 row.
Work 2 rows in SS.
Next row: K1, K2tog, knit to last 3 sts, ssk, K1 [7 sts].
Purl 1 row.
Rep last 2 rows once more [5 sts]. Cast off.

Guitar neck

For the back, cast on 4 sts in brown yarn and work 4.5cm (1¾in) in SS. Cast off.
For the front, cast on 4 sts in brown yarn and work 6cm (2¾in) in SS. Cast off.

Guitar centre

For the black centre of the guitar, use black yarn and cast on 2 sts. Knit 1 row.
Next row: P1, M1, P1.
Knit 1 row.
Next row: P1, P2tog, P1. Cast off.

Making up the guitar

Cut a guitar shape out of cardboard using the template. Sew the body piece around the shape. Sew the neck of the guitar in place, positioning the longer piece on the front of the guitar. Sew the guitar centre where the neck ends on the guitar body, shaping it into a circle as you attach it. Embroider on the details and sew four beads on to the top of the neck, using the picture for guidance.

Microphone

Using black yarn, cast on 5 sts and knit 1 row.
Next row: P1, M1, knit to last st, M1, P1 [7 sts].
Work 3 rows in SS.
Next row: P2tog, purl to last 2 sts, P2tog [5 sts].
Cast off.
Thread yarn around edge of microphone and pull tightly to make a ball shape, stuffing with toy filling.
Using black yarn, cast on 6 sts and work 6 rows in SS. Cast off. Join side seam and attach top of microphone to one end of the tube you have made. Leave a tail for the cable.

Microphone stand

Using chenille sticks, make the microphone stand shape with three legs.
Using grey yarn, cast on 5 sts and work 4 i-cords (see page 94) long enough to cover the stand and legs. Sew into place.

Any requests?

73

Hurry up! We'll be late!

Wedding Belle

Materials

White 4-ply (fingering) yarn
White sparkly 4-ply (fingering) yarn
White lace-weight yarn
Small amount of yellow 4-ply (fingering) yarn
Small amount of green embroidery thread
Bead trim
Small pearl beads

Needles

2mm (UK 14, US 0), 2.75mm (UK 12, US 2) and 3.5mm (UK 10, US 4) knitting needles
2mm (US 4) crochet hook (for scalloped edging of veil) (optional)

The pattern for the bridesmaid is on pages 82–84.

Instructions

Make adult meerkat (see pages 10–13).

Overskirt

Using 2.75mm (UK 12, US 2) needles and white 4-ply (fingering) yarn, cast on 50 sts and work 2 rows in SS.

Next row: K1, M1, knit to last st, M1, K1 [52 sts].

Purl 1 row.

Rep last 2 rows a further 8 times until there are 68 sts.

Next row: K1, (K3, K2tog) to last 2 sts, K2 [55 sts].

Purl 1 row.

Next row: K1, (K2, K2tog) to last 2 sts, K2 [42 sts].

Purl 1 row.

Next row: K2, (K2tog, K2) to end of row [32 sts].

Purl 1 row and thread a length of yarn through rem sts.

With RS of skirt facing and using white sparkly yarn, pick up and knit 18 sts along sloping edge, 35 sts along bottom edge and a further 18 sts along other sloping edge [71 sts].

Knit 1 row.

Cast off as follows:

Cast off 4 sts, (sl st back to LH needle, cast on 2 sts, cast off 5 sts) to last st, K1. This creates a picot cast off.

Underskirt

Using 2.75mm (UK 12, US 2) needles and white sparkly yarn, cast on 30 sts and work 18 rows in SS.

Next row: (K3, K2tog) to end of row [24 sts].

Purl 1 row.

Next row: (K2, K2tog) to end of row [18 sts].

Purl 1 row.

Next row: (K2, K2tog) to last 2 sts, K2 [14 sts].

Purl 1 row and thread a length of yarn through rem sts.

Bodice (make two)

Using 2.75mm (UK 12, US 2) needles and white sparkly yarn, cast on 16 sts and work 2 rows in SS.

Next row: K1, K2tog, knit to last 3 sts, ssk, K1 [14 sts].

Purl 1 row.

Can you see my tail?

Rep last 2 rows twice more [10 sts].
Cast off 2 sts at beg of next 2 rows [6 sts].
Cast off rem 6 sts.

Sleeves (make two)
Using 2.75mm (UK 12, US 2) needles and white sparkly yarn, cast on 9 sts and work 2 rows in SS.
Next row: (K1, M1) to last st, K1 [17 sts].
Purl 1 row.
Rep last 2 rows once more [33 sts].
Knit 1 row.
Next row: P2tog to last st, P1 [17 sts].
Thread a length of yarn through rem sts.

Head dress
Using 2.75mm (UK 12, US 2) needles and white sparkly yarn, cast on 2 sts and work 12 rows in SS.
Cast off.

Daisy
Follow instructions for flower on Beach Babe's bag (page 11), using white 4-ply (fingering) yarn for the flower and yellow for the centre. Make the leaves as follows:
Using 2mm (UK 14, US 0) needles and green embroidery thread, cast on 3 sts and knit 1 row.
Next row: K1, M1, K1, M1, K1 [5 sts].
Knit 3 rows.
Next row: K2tog, K1, K2tog [3 sts].
Next row: K2tog, K1 [2 sts].
K2tog and fasten off rem st.

Veil
Using white lace-weight yarn and 3.5mm (UK 10, US 4) knitting needles, cast on 8 sts and knit 1 row.
Work as follows:
Row 1: K1, (YO, K2tog) to last st, YO, K1 [9 sts].
Row 2: P1, (YO, P2tog) to end of row [9 sts].
Row 3: K1, (YO, K2tog) to end of row [9 sts].
Row 4: P1, (P2tog) to end of row [5 sts].
Row 5: YO, K1, (YO, K2tog) to end of row [6 sts].
Row 6: YO, K1, (YO, P2tog) to last st, YO, K1 [8 sts].
Row 7: YO, K1, (YO, K2tog) to last st, YO, K1 [10 sts].
Rep rows 6 and 7 until there are 32 sts, ending with a RS row.
Continue as follows:
Row 1: K1, (YO, K2tog) to last 3 sts, K3tog [30 sts].
Row 2: K1, (YO, P2tog) to last st, P1 [30 sts].
Row 3: K1, (YO, K2tog) to last st, K1 [30 sts].

Rep last 2 rows until the veil is the required length.
Next row: K1, (P2tog) to last st, K1 [16 sts].
Cast off.

Scalloped edging (optional)
Using a 2mm (US 4) crochet hook, join yarn to top LH side of veil. Join with a *US*sc/*UK*dc, make 6ch, *US*sc/*UK*dc into edge of veil to make a loop. Rep this around the veil to top RH side to make a scalloped edge.

Making up
Sew side seams of bodice and sew to top of meerkat's body. Using gathering thread, sew underskirt to front of bodice. Gather top edge of overskirt, pin in place and sew to bodice, attaching to edges of underskirt afterwards. For each sleeve, gather sleeve and sew to top of arm, attaching gathered edge to top edge of bodice.

Sew head dress to top of head and sew bead trim to top edge, making a loop in the centre. Sew veil in place behind head dress.

To make the flower, wrap a length of fine wire with green embroidery thread. Sew daisy to top of wire and attach leaves half way down using the picture as guidance.

Sew length of bead trim to join between bodice and skirt, making a loop in the middle at the front. Make necklace out of pearl beads and stitch in place. Sew 2 beads to bottom of each ear to make earrings. Sew a bead to each picot point around edge of overskirt.

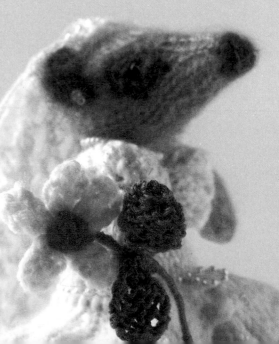

Top Hat and Tail

Materials
Dark grey 4-ply (fingering) yarn
White 4-ply (fingering) yarn
Black 4-ply (fingering) yarn
Small black button
Small amount of yellow 4-ply
   (fingering) yarn
Small amount of fine yellow ribbon
Yellow sewing cotton/embroidery
   thread to match ribbon
Sewing needle

Needles
2.75mm (UK 12, US 2)
   knitting needles

Perhaps I should
have gone on
a diet ...

The pattern for the bride is on pages 74–77.

Instructions

Make adult meerkat (see pages 10–13).

Jacket (back)

Using dark grey yarn, cast on 12 sts and work 8 rows in SS.

Cast on 3 sts at beg of next 2 rows [18 sts].

Work 2 rows.

Next row: K1, M1, knit to last st, M1, K1 [20 sts].

Work 5 rows in SS.

Next row: K10, turn.

Working over these 10 sts, work 3 rows in SS.

Next row: K1, K2tog, knit to end of row [9 sts].

Purl 1 row.

Next row: K1, K2tog, knit to end of row [8 sts].

Work 3 rows in SS.

Next row: K1, K2tog, knit to end of row [7 sts].

Purl 1 row.

Rep last 2 rows until 4 sts rem.

Cast off.

With RS facing, rejoin yarn to rem 10 sts and work as for first side, working decreases 1 st before end of row instead (shapings on outside edges).

Jacket (right front)

Using dark grey yarn, cast on 3 sts and work 4 rows in SS.

Next row: K1, M1, knit to end of row [4 sts].

Work 3 rows in SS.

Next row: K1, M1, knit to end of row [5 sts].

Cast on 3 sts at beg of next row [8 sts].

Work 6 rows in SS.

Next row: cast off 2 sts, knit to end of row [6 sts].

Purl 1 row.

Rep last 2 rows once more.

Cast off rem 4 sts.

Jacket (left front)

Using black yarn, cast on 3 sts and work 4 rows in SS.

Next row: knit to last st, M1, K1 [4 sts].

Work 3 rows in SS.

Next row: cast on 3 sts, knit to last st, M1, K1 [8 sts].

Work 7 rows in SS.

Next row: cast off 2 sts, purl to end of row [6 sts].

Knit 1 row.

Rep last 2 rows once more.

Cast off rem 4 sts.

Sleeves (make two)

Using dark grey yarn, cast on 14 sts and work 14 rows in SS. Cast off.

Collar

Using dark grey yarn, cast on 2 sts and work 4 rows in SS.

*****Next row:** K1, M1, K1 [3 sts].

Work 3 rows in SS.

Next row: K1, M1, K2 [4 sts].
Purl 1 row.*
Cast off 2 sts at beg of next row [2 sts].
Purl 1 row.
Cast on 2 sts at beg of next row [4 sts].
Purl 1 row.
Next row: K1, K2tog, K1 [3 sts].
Purl 1 row.
Next row: K1, K2tog [2 sts].
Work in SS for 6 rows.
For second half of collar, work from * to * as for first
half of collar.
Cast off 2 sts at beg of next row [2 sts].
Purl 1 row.
Cast on 2 sts at beg of next row [4 sts].
Purl 1 row.
Next row: K1, K2tog, K1 [3 sts].
Purl 1 row.
Next row: K1, K2tog [2 sts].
Work 4 rows in SS and cast off rem 2 sts.

Shirt front

Using white yarn, cast on 9 sts and work 7 rows
in SS.
Cast off 2 sts at beg of next 2 rows [5 sts].
Work 2 rows in SS.
Cast off.

Top hat

Knitted in GS.
Starting with the brim (knitted in GS) and using black
yarn, cast on 40 sts and knit 1 row.
Next row: K2tog to end of row [20 sts].
Knit 2 rows.
Next row: K2tog to end of row [10 sts].
Knit 1 row.
Next row: K2tog to end of row [5 sts].
Thread yarn through rem sts and sew seam of
brim together.
To make the top of the hat (knitted in SS), cast on
5 sts.
Next row: (K1, M1) to last st, K1 [9 sts].
Purl 1 row.
Rep last 2 rows twice more [33 sts].
Next row (RS): purl.
Starting with a purl row, work 6 rows in SS.
Cast off.

Making up

Sew shoulder and side seams of jacket. Sew shirt
front to meerkat and sew jacket together at the front,
securing to the front of the shirt. Use a small length
of ribbon to make the bow tie, securing with yellow
sewing cotton/embroidery thread.
Sew collar pieces to jacket. Sew sleeve seams and
sew to jacket.
Embroider flower using white yarn in a loopy stitch,
securing it at the centre with a French knot worked in
yellow yarn.
Sew seam of top of hat and sew to brim. Sew the top
hat to the meerkat's head.

You're the most beautiful meerkat bride EVER!

Cute Bridesmaid

Materials

White 4-ply (fingering) yarn
White sparkly 4-ply (fingering) yarn
Small amount of yellow 4-ply (fingering) yarn
Small amount of white lace-weight yarn
Small amount of fine yellow ribbon
Small amount of yellow, white and green embroidery silk
Sewing needle

Needles

2.75mm (UK 12, US 2) knitting needles
2mm (US 4) crochet hook (used for posy) (optional)

Instructions

Make baby meerkat (see pages 30–33).

Dress skirt

Using white sparkly yarn, cast on 33 sts and work 6 rows in SS.
Next row: (K3, K2tog) to last 3 sts, K3 [27 sts].
Purl 1 row.
Next row: K2, (K2 tog, K2) to last 3 sts, K3 [21 sts].
Purl 1 row.
Place sts on a length of yarn.
With RS facing and using white sparkly yarn, pick up and knit 25 sts along bottom edge of skirt.
Knit 1 row.
Cast off as follows:
Cast off 3 sts, (sl st back to LH needle, cast on 2 sts, cast off 5 sts) to end of row to make a picot edging.

Bodice

Using white sparkly yarn, cast on 14 sts and work 2 rows in SS.
Next row: K1, K2tog, knit to last 3 sts, ssk, K1 [12 sts].
Purl 1 row.
Cast off.

Sleeves (make two)

Using white sparkly yarn, cast on 7 sts.
Next row: (K1, M1) to last st, K1 [13 sts].
Work 2 rows in SS.
Thread yarn through rem sts and gather.

Posy

Using a 2mm (US 4) crochet hook and white lace-weight yarn, make 5ch and join with a sl st into first ch.
Round 2: 3ch (counts as 1*US*dc/*UK*tr), work 11*US*dc/*UK*tr into centre of circle, sl st into top of 3rd ch.
Round 3: 2*US*dc/*UK*tr into each *US*dc/*UK*tr space [24 *US*dc/*UK*tr].
Next round: 3ch, miss 1*US*dc/*UK*tr, sl st to top of next *US*dc/*UK*tr, rep to end of round and fasten off yarn.
Alternatively, use white 4-ply (fingering) yarn and 2.75mm (UK 12, US 2) knitting needles and knit a circle as for the centre of Musical Meerkat's guitar (see page 73).
Embroider flowers using embroidery silk and French knots. Attach ribbon to back of posy.

Making up

Fit bodice to meerkat and sew in place, positioning seam at centre back. Sew side seam of skirt and sew to bodice. Fit sleeves, placing gathered edge on meerkat's arm and cast-on edge on shoulder. Sew in place. Sew a length of fine yellow ribbon around the meerkat's waist using embroidery thread and make a bow at the back. Sew the posy to the meerkat's hand. Embroider head dress, as for bouquet and attach ribbon to back of head.

The Sky's the Limit

Materials

Dark brown 4-ply (fingering) yarn

Cream 4-ply (fingering) yarn

Cream lace-weight yarn (used double throughout)

Small amount of black 4-ply (fingering) yarn

Small amount of gold lace-weight yarn (used double throughout)

Small amount of toy filling

Fine wire

Needles

2.75mm (UK 12, US 2) knitting needles

stitch holder

Instructions

Make adult meerkat (see pages 10–13).

Remember to use cream and gold lace-weight yarns double throughout.

Jacket (back)

Using brown yarn, cast on 12 sts and work 8 rows in SS.

Cast on 3 sts at beg of next 2 rows [18 sts].

Work 2 rows.

Next row: K1, M1, knit to last st, M1, K1 [20 sts].

Work 7 rows in SS.

Change to double strand of cream lace-weight yarn and knit to end of row.

Next row (WS): starting with a knit row, work 5 rows in rev SS. Cast off.

Jacket (right front)

Using brown yarn, cast on 5 sts and work 8 rows in SS.

Cast on 3 sts at beg of next row.

Work 3 rows.

Next row: K1, M1, knit to end of row [9 sts].

Work 7 rows in SS.

Change to cream lace-weight yarn and purl to end of row.

Next row (WS): starting with a knit row, work 5 rows in rev SS. Cast off.

Pick up and knit 11 sts using the cream lace-weight yarn to start of shaping. Cast off.

Jacket (left front)

Using brown yarn, cast on 5 sts and work 9 rows in SS.

Cast on 3 sts at beg of next row (WS) [8 sts].

Work 2 rows.

Next row: knit to last st, M1, K1 [9 sts].

Work 7 rows in SS.

Change to cream lace-weight yarn and knit to end of row.

Next row (WS): starting with a knit row, work 5 rows in rev SS. Cast off.

Sleeves (make two)

Using brown yarn, cast on 14 sts and work 8 rows in SS. Change to cream lace-weight yarn and knit to end of row.

Starting with a knit row, work 5 rows in rev SS. Cast off.

Collar (make two)

Using a double strand of cream lace-weight yarn, cast on 2 sts and knit 1 row.

Next row: K1, M1, knit to end of row [3 sts].

Knit 1 row.

Rep last 2 rows once more [5 sts].

Knit 2 rows.

Cast off 3 sts at beg of next row [2 sts].

Knit 1 row.

Cast on 3 sts at beg of foll row [5 sts].

Knit 1 row.

Next row: K1, K2tog, knit to end of row [4 sts].

Knit 1 row.

Rep last 2 rows once more [3 sts].

Continue to work in GS over rem 3 sts until collar is long enough to reach to back of neck.

Scarf

Using cream 4-ply (fingering) yarn, cast on 8 sts and work 20 rows in SS.

Next row: K1, K2tog, K2, ssk, K1 [6 sts].

Continue in SS until work measures 10cm (4in).

Next row: K1, M1, knit to last st, M1, K1 [8 sts].
Work 20 rows in SS. Cast off.

Chin straps (make two)
Using brown yarn, cast on 2 sts and work 6 rows in SS.
Next row: K1, M1, K1 [3 sts].
Purl 1 row.
Next row: (K1, M1) twice, K1 [5 sts].
Work 3 rows in SS. Place sts on a holder.

Hat
Join chin straps and start main part of hat as follows:
Using brown yarn, cast on 4 sts, turn.
Knit along 5 sts of first chin strap, turn.
Cast on 10 sts, turn.
Knit along 5 sts of second chin strap, turn.
Cast on 4 sts [28 sts].
Starting with a purl row, work 3 rows in SS.
Next row: (K2, K2tog) to end of row [21 sts].
Purl 1 row.
Next row: K2tog to last st, K1 [11 sts].
Next row: P2tog to last st, P1 [6 sts].
Thread yarn through rem sts.

Ear defenders (make two)
Using brown yarn, cast on 3 sts and work 2 rows in SS.
Next row: K1, M1, K1, M1, K1 [5 sts].
Work 3 rows In SS.
Next row: K2tog, K1, ssk [3 sts].
Purl 1 row.
Cast off.

Goggles (make two)
Using black yarn, cast on 1 st and inc by Kfbf into st [3 sts].
Work 3 rows in SS.
Next row: sl1, K2tog, psso [1 st].
Fasten off rem st.

Moustache
Work as for Santa Paws' moustache (page 45) using gold lace-weight yarn.

Making up
Sew shoulder seams of jacket and fit to the meerkat. Sew side seams and sew front edges together. Sew sleeve seams and sew into place.

Sew collar on to jacket, joining at back of neck.
Sew hat on to meerkat's head and sew ear defenders in place on to chin straps, stuffing them slightly with toy filling. Sew goggles on to top of head and embroider between each goggle and either side of goggles in chain stitch, using the picture as guidance.
Sew moustache just underneath the meerkat's nose.
Place fine wire around the edge of the scarf and oversew in place using cream 4-ply (fingering) yarn. Wrap around the meerkat's neck.

Prehistoric Kat

Oh no, I'm stuck!

K1, K2tog, knit to end of row [9 sts].
Next row (WS): K6, P3.
This row forms the top of the dinosaur's head.
K1, M1, knit to end of row [10 sts].
Cast off 2 sts, purl to end of row [8 sts].
K1, M1, knit to end of row [9 sts].
Cast off 4 sts, purl to end of row [5 sts].
Knit 1 row.
Purl 1 row.
K1, M1, knit to end of row [6 sts].
Cast on 4 sts, purl to end of row [10 sts].
Work 3 rows in SS.
Cast off 3 sts, purl to end of row [7 sts].
Knit 1 row.
Cast on 3 sts, purl to end of row [10 sts].
Work 4 rows in SS.
Next row: K1, M1, knit to end of row [11 sts].
Purl 1 row.
Rep these 2 rows 3 more times [14 sts].
Cast on 3 sts, knit to end of row [17 sts].
Cast off 2 sts, purl to end of row [15 sts].
Cast on 4 sts, knit to end of row [19 sts].
Purl 1 row.
Cast off.

Bottom jaw
Using green yarn, cast on 5 sts and knit 1 row.
Cast on 2 sts at beg of next row [7 sts].
Work 3 rows in SS.
Cast off 2 sts at beg of next row [5 sts].
Knit 1 row.
Cast off rem sts.

Eyes
Using green yarn, cast on 5 sts and work 6 rows in GS.
Cast off. Fold so that cast-on and cast-off edges are together and, using white and black yarn, embroider eyes in place using the picture as guidance.

Spine
Using green yarn, cast on 1 st and knit 1 row.
Cast on 1 st, K1 [2 sts].
*Knit 1 row.
Cast on 1 st, K2 [3 sts].
Knit 1 row.

Instructions
Make baby meerkat (see pages 30–33).

Dinosaur costume
Worked in one piece from bottom.
Using green yarn, cast on 19 sts and work 2 rows in SS.
Cast off 4 sts, knit to end of row [15 sts].
Cast on 2 sts, purl to end of row [17 sts].
Cast off 3 sts, knit to end of row [14 sts].
Purl 1 row.
Next row: K1, K2tog, knit to end of row [13 sts].
Purl 1 row.
Rep last 2 rows 3 more times [10 sts].
Work 3 rows in SS.
Cast off 3 sts, purl to end of row [7 sts].
Knit 1 row.
Cast on 3 sts, purl to end of row [10 sts].
Work 3 rows in SS.
Cast off 4 sts, purl to end of row [6 sts].
K1, K2tog, knit to end of row [5 sts].
Purl 1 row.
Knit 1 row.
Cast on 4 sts, purl to end of row [9 sts].
K1, K2tog, knit to end of row [8 sts].
Cast on 2 sts, purl to end of row [10 sts].

Cast on 1 st, K3 [4 sts].
Knit 1 row.
Cast off 3 sts.*
Rep from * to * until you have enough spines to go
down the back and tail of the dinosaur.
Cast off rem st.

Making up

With RS together (WS is on the outside), sew dinosaur
costume together from end of tail to back of head.
Fit round meerkat and sew seams above and
below arms.
Sew eyes to top of dinosaur's head.
Using white yarn, embroider French knots on top and
bottom jaw to make teeth.
Sew bottom jaw in place.
Sew spine in place along back seam.

Techniques

I-cord

To make an i-cord, cast on your stitches using a double-pointed needle, knit them and slide to the other end of the same needle. Pull the yarn across the back of the needle and knit the stitches again. Repeat these instructions until the cord is long enough. By pulling the yarn behind the stitches on the needle, you close the 'gap' and give the appearance of French knitting. Alternatively, you can work the stitches in stocking stitch and sew up the seam.

French knots

Bring the sewing needle through to the front of the work and wind the yarn around the needle twice. Take the needle through the work, half a stitch away, holding the loops around the needle with your fingers while pulling the yarn through to the back of your work. Fasten off.

Here are some of the materials you need: 4-ply (fingering) yarn; knitting needles; narrow ribbon; chenille sticks; tiny buttons and beads.

Mattress stitch

This is a really neat way to join two pieces of stocking stitch together. The seam is practically invisible and not at all bulky. Begin by laying the work side by side with the right side facing you. Slip your needle through the horizontal bar between the first and second stitch of the first row on one piece and then repeat this process on the opposite piece. Work back and forth up this line of stitches for about 2.5cm (1in). Gently pull the yarn in the direction of the seam (upwards) and you will see the two sets of stitches join together. Repeat this process until you reach the top of the seam.

Wrap and turn

This technique ensures you do not end up with a 'hole' in your knitting when working short row shaping and turning your work mid-row. Slip the following stitch from the left to the right needle. Move the yarn from the back to the front of the work, between the needles. Slip stitch back to the right-hand needle. Turn work.

Backstitch

Bring the threaded needle from the back to the front of the knitting. Form a stitch by taking the needle back through approximately 5mm (¼in) behind where your thread has come through (in the opposite direction to your stitching). Bring it back through to the right side of the knitting approximately 5mm (¼in) in front of the stitch (in the same direction as your stitching). Repeat.

Blanket stitch

Thread a darning needle with yarn and bring to the front of your work as close as possible to the edge. Take the needle to the back about 1cm (½in) along and approximately 1cm (½in) from the edge, and bring it back to the front at the edge of the knitting. Loop your yarn under the needle and pull it though until it lays neatly against the emerging yarn. Repeat this process.

Abbreviations

Knitting abbreviations

alt	alternate	psso	pass slipped stitch over
beg	beginning	rem	remaining
cm	centimetres	rep	repeat
dec	decrease	rev	reverse
foll	following	rev SS	reverse stocking stitch, i.e. knit the sts on the WS
GS	garter stitch		and purl the sts on the RS
inc	increase	RS	right side
K	knit	skpo	slip 1, knit 1, pass slipped stitch over
K2tog	knit 2 stitches together	sl	slip a stitch
Kfb	knit into front and back of stitch	SM	slip marker from left to right needle
	(increasing one stitch)	SS	stocking stitch
Kfbf	knit into front, back and front of stitch	ssk	slip 2 sts knitwise one at a time, pass the 2
	(increasing two stitches)		slipped sts back to left needle, knit both together
M	marker		through back of loop
M1	make a backwards loop on needle by twisting	ssp	slip 2 sts knitwise one at a time, pass 2 slipped
	yarn towards you and slipping resulting loop on to		sts back to left needle, purl 2 slipped sts together
	right-hand needle. On following row, knit or purl		from back, left to right
	through back of stitch. This produces a very	st(s)	stitch(es)
	neat result	tbl	through the back of the loop
P	purl	tog	together
P2tog	purl 2 stitches together	w&t	wrap and turn (see techniques)
Pfb	purl into front and back of stitch	WS	wrong side
	(increasing one stitch)	yo	yarn over needle
PM	place marker	yrn	yarn round needle

UK/US crochet abbreviations

American and British crochet terms differ, as shown in
the table below. In the patterns in this book, both US
and UK terms are provided.

US		UK	
ch	chain	ch	chain
sc	single crochet	dc	double crochet
dc	double crochet	tr	treble crochet
sl st	slip stitch	sl st	slip stitch